It's a Small World
Felted Friends

Cute and Cuddly Needle Felted Figures
from Around the World

Sachiko Susa

TUTTLE Publishing

Tokyo │ Rutland, Vermont │ Singapore

CONTENTS

INSTRUCTIONS ON PAGES 42–43

I've made a little world from the kingdom of felt. With each piece I made, the world grew larger, and I felt as if I were on a fun journey. A needle transforms roving into all kinds of shapes. It's not limited to animals and people—it lends itself to things like houses, castles and scenery too. I hope you'll enjoy experiencing the gentle sweetness and warmth of wool felt in these pieces.

Sachiko Susa

NETHERLANDS

Girl and Windmill INSTRUCTIONS ON PAGES 43–45

The window sills of houses in the Netherlands are decorated with
flowers all year round. From among the prettily blooming tulips,
a smiling girl greets people passing by. "Welcome to the Netherlands!"

Hallo

CHINA

Three Panda Brothers INSTRUCTIONS ON PAGES 46–47

As China's ambassador of friendship, the giant panda delights people everywhere. Rolling and spinning in circles, the panda could well be the most adorable creature in the whole world. These pampered, slightly fussy brothers love to play.

nǐ hǎo

AUSTRALIA

Mother and Baby Koala   INSTRUCTIONS ON PAGES 48–49

The koala is an animal found only in Australia. Surprisingly, it gets all its nutrients exclusively from eucalyptus leaves. But this baby koala is still feeding on its mother's milk.

G'day

 # AUSTRALIA

Mother Kangaroo and Joey INSTRUCTIONS ON PAGES 50–51

In Australia the kangaroo is a familiar sight. A little joey will stay snug in its mama's pouch for months before starting to wander about on its own.

NEW ZEALAND

Sheep on a Hill INSTRUCTIONS ON PAGE 52

New Zealand is blessed with a wealth of nature, and animals and humans co-exist in this spiritually rich country. This figure expresses gratitude for the gift of the wool that's produced from New Zealand's healthily-raised sheep.

RUSSIA

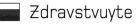

Four Matryoshka Maidens INSTRUCTIONS ON PAGE 53

Think Russian souvenirs, think Matryoshka dolls. Their appeal lies in their simplicity, which shines through in the warmth inherent in handmade objects. Aren't these four maidens a bunch of beauties?

Hamburger and Donut Dangles   INSTRUCTIONS ON PAGES 54–55

Fast food is synonymous with American cuisine. American fast food is unmatched in terms of volume, but can't be beaten for its flavor and appearance either. Making this little burger, donut and drinks is "fast" too!

MEXICO

Monkey with Maracas and Cactus INSTRUCTIONS ON PAGES 56–59

Pass through the wild desert of densely growing cacti and you're greeted by a cheerful monkey! Take a few minutes out from an adventurous journey to get acquainted.

Hola

post mail

INDIA

Elephant on Festival Day INSTRUCTIONS ON PAGES 60–61

As the first signs of spring emerge, a northern Indian city stages the elephant festival. In India, the elephant is a god that brings luck as well as prosperity in business. During the festival, elephants are decorated—and celebrated!

Namaste

PALAU

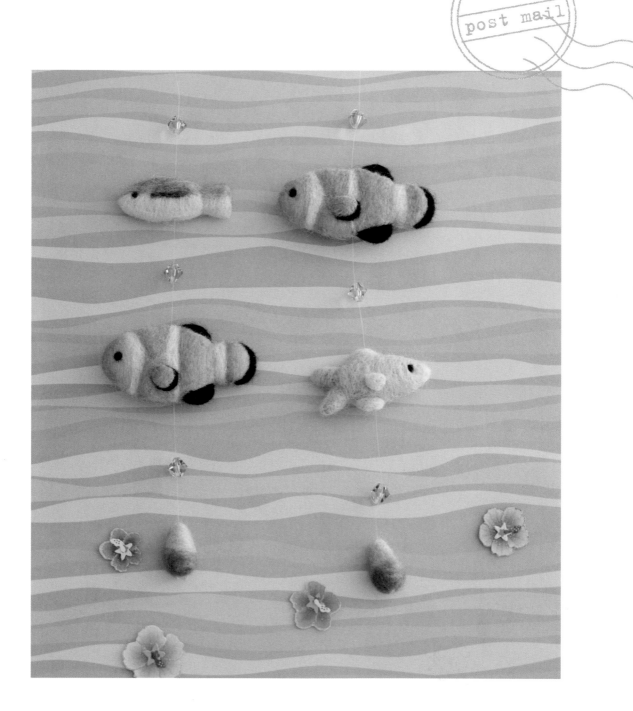

Tropical Fish Mobile INSTRUCTIONS ON PAGE 62

In the limitless blue and quiet of the ocean, all kinds of life flourish. They may not exchange words, but these colorful fish still get their message of warm welcome across. Their swaying movement makes them appear to be swimming, creating a sense of deep relaxation.

Alli

Rabbit Gondolier and His Gondola INSTRUCTIONS ON PAGES 63–65

Canals of all different sizes spread across Venice like a web. On this romantic trip, the pilot is a handsome rabbit, steering through the maze of the city on a gently rocking gondola.

post mail

FINLAND

Santa Claus with Gifts INSTRUCTIONS ON PAGES 66–69

When it comes to the world's happiest counties, Finland generally ranks high on the list. No doubt Santa, who lives in Finland year-round, has something to do with that! As they do every year, children around the world are waiting for his delivery of presents.

24

 Hyvääpäivää

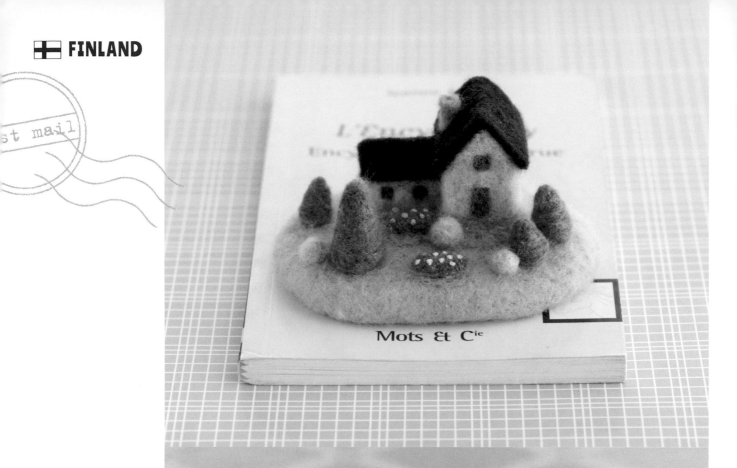

╋ FINLAND

Little House in Spring and Winter   INSTRUCTIONS ON PAGES 70–72

Surrounded by forest, wooden houses are traditional dwellings in Finland. They are
built with simplicity and are snug and comfortable whether the season is warm or cold.

CANADA

Bear in the Forest INSTRUCTIONS ON PAGE 76

Canada is the second largest country in the world.
Its cities are all surrounded by beautiful nature, and outdoor
activities can be enjoyed to the fullest. This mischievous bear
is waiting in the woods. Do you want to go skiing? Or trekking?

GERMANY

Teddy Bears and Castle   INSTRUCTIONS ON PAGES 73–75

Germany represents Europe's special kind of refinement through everything from ancient castles to little bears. It's been more than 130 years since the birth of the teddy bear. Its original creator, the Steiff company, produced each bear by hand and distinguished their brand by sewing a button into the ear.

 Guten tag

FRANCE

Paris Dangle   INSTRUCTIONS ON PAGE 77

Also known as the Iron Lady, the Eiffel Tower has lots of renditions, including
this fleecy strap. What do you think of the softest Eiffel Tower in the world?

UNITED KINGDOM

London Dangle   INSTRUCTIONS ON PAGES 78–79

Steeped in serious history, London is also an exciting city that sets trends around the world. Here, the straitlaced guards charged with protecting the Queen get a charming makeover. Anything goes in this captivating, cutting-edge city.

A Little Journey Around the World
... in the Palm of Your Hand

It's so easy to take a little trip around the world.

Let your imagination take flight. Look back on the countries you've been to or think of the countries you'd like to visit, and start felting.

As you gaze at the creation in your hand, your heart will soar to new places around the world.

33

Kinds of Wool Felt   Wool roving used for these projects

Colors used for the projects in this book have been given general names for reference purposes and do not correspond to any particular brand of roving. Use the color chart to guide your selections. You can also substitute these colors and/or types of wool roving with any others of your choosing.

Solid This is a versatile wool for felting and can be used for a wide variety of projects. It also comes in a wide array of colors. Colors used in these projects include the following:

| White | Pale Yellow | Primary Yellow | Lemon Yellow | Orange Yellow | Dark Orange | Pale Pink |

| Salmon | Rose | Deep Red | Lilac | Purple | Light Blue | Sky Blue |

| Robin's Egg Blue | Primary Blue | Navy Blue | Green | Leaf Green | Pale Green | Spring Green |

| Moss Green | Wheat | Brown | Deep Brown | Black |

Mixed Some projects include roving of fibers that have been blended for a heathery texture and tone. Look for blended roving in these colors:

| Golden | Pink | Green | Moss | Chestnut | Rich Brown | Slate Blue |

Natural fine Merino Blends of British and Merino wools. These have a wide variety of felting applications.

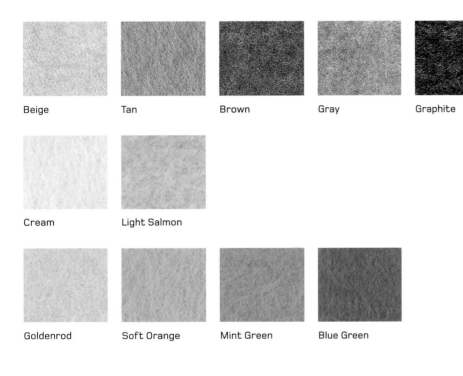

Beige   Tan   Brown   Gray   Graphite

Cream   Light Salmon

Goldenrod   Soft Orange   Mint Green   Blue Green

Prefelted Wool Comes in sheet form but is not fully felted. Rather, it's loose enough to be cut or torn, then applied and felted to the surface of your figures.

French Vanilla   Soft Green   White

Unbleached   Beige   Camel

Other types of wool used in these projects include:

Shetland Roving This roving is easy to felt. In its unbleached form it adds a nice, natural off-white color.

Felting Yarn Loop A felting yarn from the Hamanaka company in Japan, this is available online and in some craft stores. It is excellent for making curly-haired animals such as sheep.

Natural White Merino This is used in a few of the projects in this book. This is a soft fiber, so felting it firmly can take some time, but it results in a wonderful surface.

Batting This is less expensive than roving and can be lightly punched to form a good core or base for most projects.

Making a Castle with Base INSTRUCTIONS ON PAGES 74–75

Also see "Choosing the Needle" and "Finished Firmess" on p41.

BASE

1 A felting mat is used as a work surface when punching into felt with a needle, but for this project it will be used to form a base.

2 Using thick card as the template, trace the shape of the base onto the felting mat with a ballpoint pen.

3 Use a box cutter to cut to a width of about ⅜ in (8mm), then trim edges from around the top only.

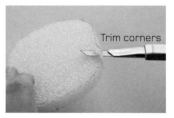

4 The completed base foundation.

5 Cut prefelted sheet to a suitable size to wrap the base.

6 With the top surface of the mat facing down, gather edges of the prefelted sheet in the center of the mat's underside and punch in to secure in place.

7 Use scissors to trim off excess from the sheet.

8 Work the needle over the entire piece so the prefelted sheet won't peel off.

HOUSE WITH PITCHED ROOF

9 Cut felting mat into house shape.

10 Wrap with prefelted sheet.

11 Trim off excess from the sheet with scissors and smooth out by punching with the needle.

12 Wrap with prefelted sheet the other way and punch in.

13 Repeat wrapping three times. If the corners become too rounded, add roving and adjust shape.

14 For the roof, tear off bits of roving and punch them in a little at a time.

TOWER

15 Cut prefelted sheet to the width of the tower.

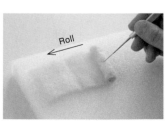

16 Punch in, rolling tightly as you go.

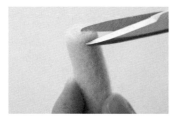

17 Trim around one end to form a conical shape.

18 The trimmed shape.

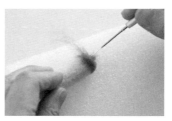

19 Tear off some roving and add a little at a time to form the tip of the tower.

20 Punch in windows, making sure the corners are defined.

ASSEMBLY

21 The completed individual parts.

22 Use craft glue to join parts together.

23 Apply craft glue to underside of castle and attach to base.

(Try making your own original designs)

SHRUBBERY

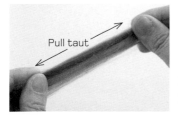

24 To blend two colors of roving, pull taut and tear.

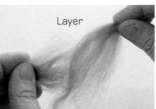

Layer

25 Layer roving.

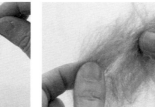

26 Pull taut and layer roving repeatedly.

29 The completed project.

27 Tear off an appropriate amount and punch into shape on the mat.

28 Arrange densely around the castle.

Making a Teddy Bear INSTRUCTIONS ON PAGE 73

Also see "Choosing the Needle" and "Finished Firmness" on p41.

CREATE INDIVIDUAL PARTS

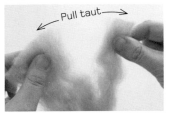

← Pull taut →

1 For each part, pull apart roving using your hands, not scissors.

Form into a ball

2 For the body and head, roll into a round shape, punching with the needle as you go.

3 Form a leg shape.

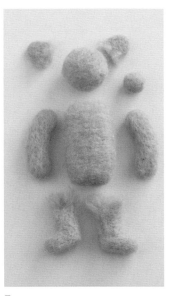

4 Wind roving around to create volume.

5 Leave the leg joint section fluffy.

6 Leave the base of the ears fluffy.

7 Make the arms teddy bear-like by firming them up rather than leaving them fluffy.

ASSEMBLY

8 Join the head and body by punching with the needle.

9 Cover with roving from the head down and over the body.

10 Punch over the join so that it isn't noticeable.

11 Wrap the roving around horizontally and punch in.

12 Add a dark shade of roving to the soles of the feet.

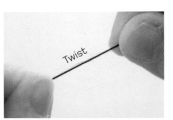

Twist

13 Twist a small amount of roving into a fine thread for the claws.

CLAWS

14 Carefully punch in roving to create lines.

15 Trim off excess with scissors.

16 Attach legs at right angles to body. Layer roving over the join so it is less visible.

17 Attach legs in a seated position.

18 Attach arms to body with craft glue.

19 When glue is dry, punch the area with the needle.

20 Make sure facial joins are not obvious.

21 Spread out the fluffy section at the base of the ears.

22 Add roving for a natural join.

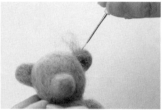

23 Add dark colored roving to the ears.

FACE

24 Work roving on the felting mat to form the nose.

25 Decide on the positioning of the eyes and create holes using an awl.

26 Apply glue to the ends of the eyes and insert into holes.

27 For the mouth, twist roving and punch in carefully as if drawing a line.

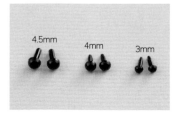

4.5mm 4mm 3mm

Plastic eyes come in a number of sizes. The sizes above are well suited to small figures.

Projects involving eyes will also involve an awl.
Craft glue is used in a number of projects for bonding eyes, joining individual parts and applying embellishments. So be sure to keep an awl and a bottle of your favorite craft glue handy.

Place the arms however you like.

Multi-purpose Dangle

See "Choosing the Needle" and "Finished Firmness" on p41.

CREATE THE BASE SHAPE

1 Lightly punch batting.

2 It's easily worked into shape so is convenient for forming a base.

3 Add the details to the figure you will be attaching to the strap.

4 Using doubled thread, pass the needle through from bottom to top.

5 A long, sturdy needle such as a mattress needle is ideal.

6 Thread the strap on.

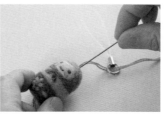

7 Pass the needle back through the head, at the same point from which it emerged.

8 Bring the needle out at the same point that it entered.

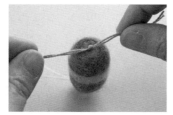

9 Tie thread in a reef knot.

10 Cut thread.

11 Punch in roving to conceal knot.

12 The completed strap.

So easy, you'll want to make a bunch!

Use good strong thread when making these dangles.

Before Starting Your Wool Felting Journey

CHOOSING THE NEEDLE
There are various types of needle, including single and double-point types. A single needle is most commonly used. The double or triple-point needle types allow for work to be completed more quickly. Needles also vary in thickness, with fine needles used to complete projects while thick needles are suited for creating separate parts. Patterned or cushioned needles can be used comfortably for long periods, so are ideal for long projects.

THE TRICK TO NEEDLE FELTING
When I work the needle into wool felt, I make an effort to be slow and careful, as working quickly is tiring. It also increases the risk of pricking your finger, so it's best to work in a relaxed manner and take things slowly.

FINISHED FIRMNESS
Wool becomes firmer the more it is needle felted. Adjust the firmness depending on what you are making. In general, it is fine to work until you are satisfied with the degree of firmness, but pieces such as phone strap figures that are carried around should be felted firmly. Animals' legs support their bodies so these also need to be firm.

SEWING AND EMBROIDERING
Some projects require a little sewing or embroidering, and it is always good to have a needle and thread handy in any case. For sewing seed beads, embroidering and attaching other embellishments, a slim needle works well for these projects. For stringing through entire felted figures, a strong, long needle—and doubled thread—will be needed.

Please note that size measurements are given in both inches and metrics. Metric measurements are more precise. Weights are given in grams. Approximate ounce equivalents can be found in the table below. All weights given are guidelines only.

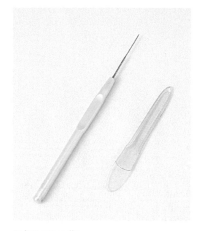

Felting Needle
My favorite needle

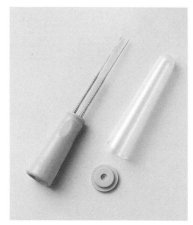

Felting Needle Holder
Made so needles can be interchanged. A double-point type allows for faster felting.

GRAMS	OZ	GRAMS	OZ
1g	0.035 oz	9g	0.32 oz
1.5g	0.053 oz	10g	0.35 oz
2g	0.07 oz	12g	0.42 oz
3g	0.1 oz	14g	0.49 oz
4g	0.14 oz	15g	0.53 oz
5g	0.18 oz	16g	0.56 oz
6g	0.21 oz	18g	0.63 oz
7g	0.25 oz	26g	0.92 oz
8g	0.28 oz		

Bear Holding Flags of the World

Page 3

Bear...height 2½ in (6.5cm)
MATERIALS
Felting wool
Natural blend: tan 5g, small amount of beige
Solid: small amounts of brown, robin's egg blue
Extras: solid black eyes, 3mm x 1 set
Have handy: awl, glue

Balloons...height 2⅜ in (6cm) incl. cord
MATERIALS
Felting wool, natural blend: goldenrod 1g, mint green 1g, light salmon 1.5g,
Solid: white 1g
Extras: thick monofilament cord x 6 in (15cm) cut into 3 lengths

<ACTUAL-SIZE PARTS>
○ Figures indicate number of parts required
Use tan unless otherwise indicated

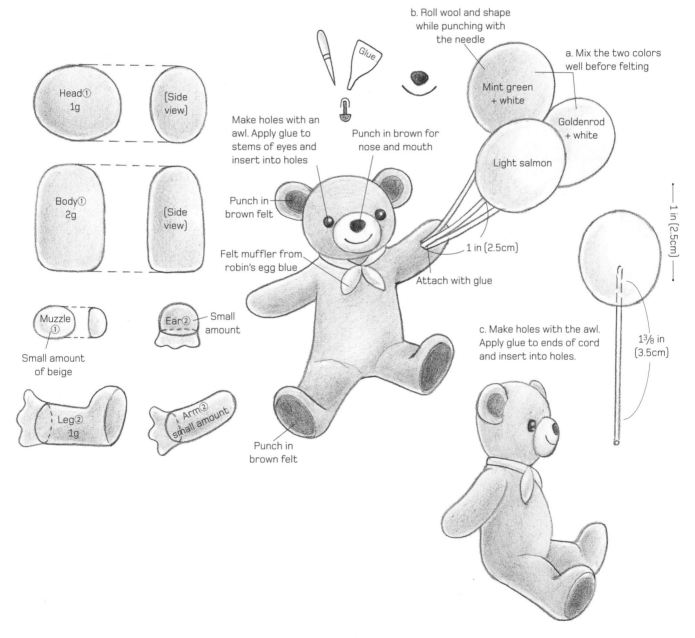

Head① 1g

(Side view)

Body① 2g

(Side view)

Muzzle ①

Small amount of beige

Ear② Small amount

Leg② 1g

Arm② small amount

Punch in brown felt

b. Roll wool and shape while punching with the needle

Glue

a. Mix the two colors well before felting

Mint green + white

Goldenrod + white

Light salmon

Make holes with an awl. Apply glue to stems of eyes and insert into holes

Punch in brown for nose and mouth

Punch in brown felt

Felt muffler from robin's egg blue

1 in (2.5cm)

Attach with glue

Punch in brown felt

c. Make holes with the awl. Apply glue to ends of cord and insert into holes.

1 in (2.5cm)

1⅜ in (3.5cm)

National Flags...⁷⁄₈ x ⁵⁄₈ in (2x1.5cm)

MATERIALS

Felting wool

Solid: small amounts of white, deep red, primary blue, robin's egg blue, leaf green, primary yellow, black

Extras: thick monofilament cord 6¼ in (16cm)

Have handy: glue

Instructions for bear

1. Create individual parts, referring to actual-size diagrams
2. Attach head to body
3. Attach limbs
4. Attach muzzle to face and create facial features (eyes, nose, mouth)
5. Attach ears
6. Attach muffler
7. Place balloons and flags in bear's paw

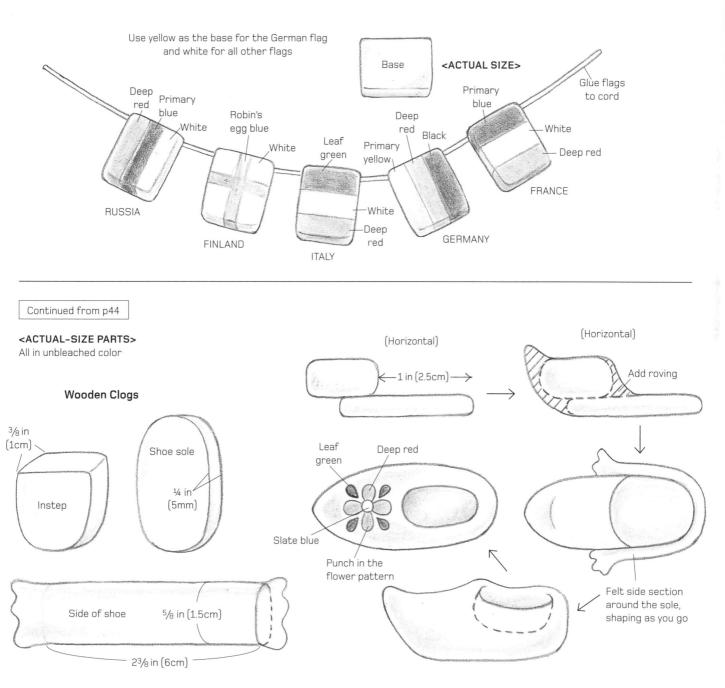

Use yellow as the base for the German flag and white for all other flags

Base

<ACTUAL SIZE>

Glue flags to cord

Deep red / Primary blue / White

Robin's egg blue / White

Leaf green

Deep red / Primary yellow / White / Deep red

Black / Primary blue

Primary blue / White / Deep red

RUSSIA

FINLAND

ITALY

GERMANY

FRANCE

Continued from p44

<ACTUAL-SIZE PARTS>
All in unbleached color

Wooden Clogs

³⁄₈ in (1cm)

Instep

Shoe sole

¼ in (5mm)

Side of shoe   ⁵⁄₈ in (1.5cm)

2³⁄₈ in (6cm)

(Horizontal)

←1 in (2.5cm)→

(Horizontal)

Add roving

Leaf green

Deep red

Slate blue

Punch in the flower pattern

Felt side section around the sole, shaping as you go

NETHERLANDS
Girl and Windmill
Page 4

Wooden Clogs—length 2 in (5cm)
MATERIALS
Felting wool
Unbleached Shetland x 5g
Solid: small amounts of deep red, leaf
green
Mixed: small amount of slate blue

Girl…height 3⅞ in (9.5cm)
MATERIALS
Felting wool
Unbleached Shetland x 15g
Natural blend: cream x 5g, small
amount of light salmon
Solid: small amounts of deep red,
black, leaf green
Mixed: small amounts of rich brown ,
slate blue
Extras: set of solid black eyes, 3mm
diameter

Instructions
1. Create individual parts, referring
   to actual-size diagrams
2. Attach head to body
3. Work indicated colors into body
4. Attach hands
5. Felt bonnet to head and attach
   bangs and braids
6. Attach ornamental flaps to both
   sides of bonnet. Glue bottom
   wing tips to hat.
7. Create face (eyes, eyebrows,
   mouth, nose)

<ACTUAL–SIZE PARTS>
◯ Figures indicate number of parts required

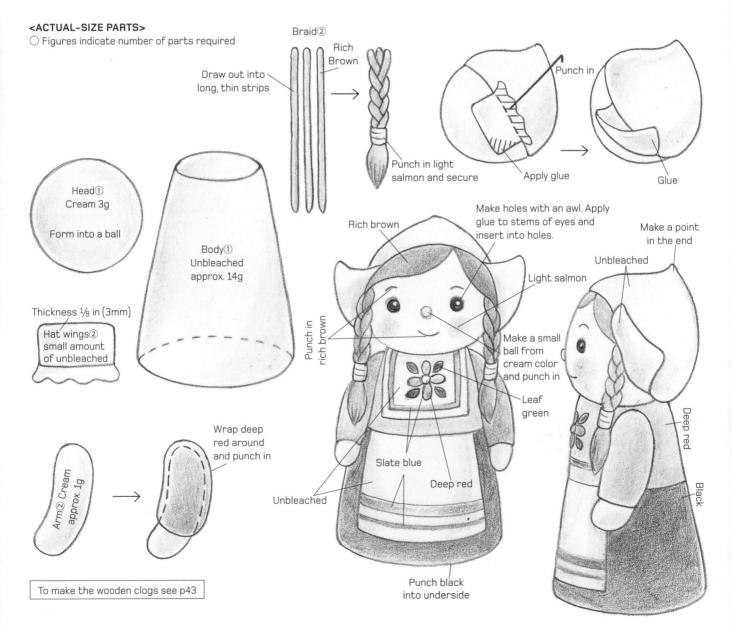

Braid②
Rich Brown

Draw out into long, thin strips

Punch in light salmon and secure

Punch in

Apply glue

Glue

Head① Cream 3g
Form into a ball

Body① Unbleached approx. 14g

Thickness ⅛ in (3mm)

Hat wings② small amount of unbleached

Make holes with an awl. Apply glue to stems of eyes and insert into holes.

Rich brown

Light salmon

Make a point in the end

Unbleached

Punch in rich brown

Make a small ball from cream color and punch in

Leaf green

Slate blue

Deep red

Unbleached

Deep red

Black

Arm② Cream approx. 1g

Wrap deep red around and punch in

Punch black into underside

To make the wooden clogs see p43

44

Windmill...height 2⅜ in (6cm), length 3¾ in (9.5cm)

MATERIALS

Felting wool

Prefelted sheet, solid: soft green 6 x 5⅛ in (15x13cm)

Prefelted sheet, mixed: camel 1½ x 4 in (4x10cm)

Small amounts of each of the colors below:

Natural blend: beige, graphite

Solid: brown, leaf green, pale yellow

Mixed: moss

Extras: felting mat 4 x 2⅜ in (10x6cm)

Thick monofilament cord 2⅜ in (6cm)

Small amounts of no. 25 embroidery thread in rose,
   light pink, white

Commercially available felt sheet in brown, ⅜ x ⅜ in (9x9mm)

Have handy: glue, trimmer, scissors, sewing/embroidery
   needle

Instructions

1. Create individual parts, referring to actual-size
   diagrams
2. Create base (see p36)
3. Create windmill
   a. Use camel-colored prefelted sheet for the body
      of the windmill
   b. Punch in brown for the roof and windows
   c. Create blades and attach to body of the windmill
      with glue
4. Embroider flower beds
5. Attach windmill to base with glue. Punch in finely cut
   soft green prefelted sheet to cover joins (see p71)
6. Glue trees, shrubs and flower beds to base

<ACTUAL-SIZE PARTS>

○ Figures indicate number of parts required

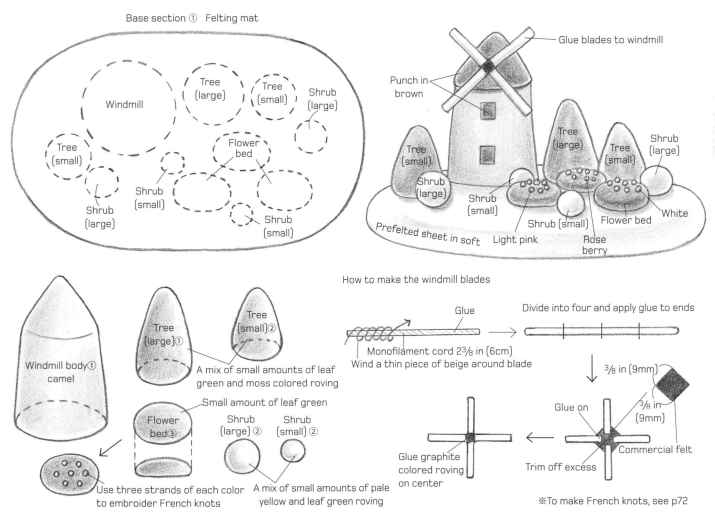

Base section ① Felting mat

Windmill · Tree (large) · Tree (small) · Shrub (large) · Tree (small) · Flower bed · Shrub (large) · Shrub (small) · Shrub (small)

Glue blades to windmill

Punch in brown

Tree (small) · Tree (large) · Tree (small) · Shrub (large)

Shrub (large) · Shrub (small) · Shrub (small) · Flower bed · White

Prefelted sheet in soft · Light pink · Rose berry

Windmill body① camel

Tree (large)① · Tree (small)②

A mix of small amounts of leaf green and moss colored roving

Small amount of leaf green

Flower bed③ · Shrub (large) ② · Shrub (small) ②

Use three strands of each color to embroider French knots

A mix of small amounts of pale yellow and leaf green roving

How to make the windmill blades

Glue

Monofilament cord 2⅜ in (6cm)
Wind a thin piece of beige around blade

Divide into four and apply glue to ends

⅜ in (9mm)

Glue on

⅜ in (9mm)

Commercial felt

Trim off excess

Glue graphite colored roving on center

※To make French knots, see p72

45

CHINA
Three Panda Brothers
Page 6

Panda…length 3⅛ in (8cm)
MATERIALS (for one panda)
Felting wool
Natural merino: white 7g
Solid: black 5g
Extras: set of solid black eyes,
  3mm diameter

Felt ball…diameter ⅞ in (2cm)
MATERIALS
Felting wool
Solid: small amounts of rose,
  primary yellow
Have handy: awl, glue

Instructions
1. Create individual parts, referring to actual-size diagrams
2. Attach head to body
3. Attach front and hind legs to body
4. Attach muzzle to face and create facial features
5. Attach ears to head
6. Attach tail to body
7. Work in black roving to areas on ears, legs and back that should be black

<ACTUAL-SIZE PARTS>
○ Figures indicate number of parts required
Use white unless otherwise indicated
Make each panda the same way apart from the legs

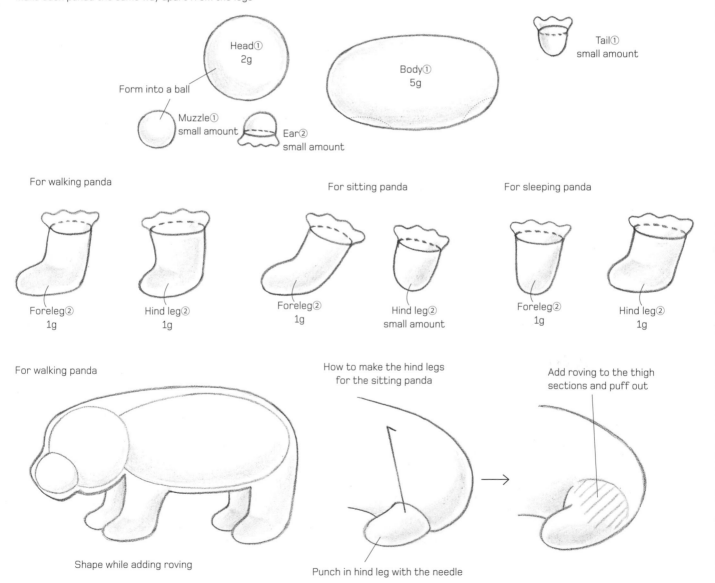

Head① 2g
Form into a ball
Muzzle① small amount
Ear② small amount
Body① 5g
Tail① small amount

For walking panda
Foreleg② 1g
Hind leg② 1g

For sitting panda
Foreleg② 1g
Hind leg② small amount

For sleeping panda
Foreleg② 1g
Hind leg② 1g

For walking panda
Shape while adding roving

How to make the hind legs for the sitting panda
Punch in hind leg with the needle

Add roving to the thigh sections and puff out

Walking panda

Punch in black around the eyes

(Rear view)

Tail

Make holes with an awl. Apply glue to stems of eyes and insert into holes.

Punch in nose and mouth using black

Glue

Attach head on at a slight angle

Sitting panda

(Back view)

Round out the back

Sleeping panda

Attach arms so the paws face each other

Attach legs the same way

AUSTRALIA
Mother and Baby Koala
Page 8

Mother and Baby Koala…height: 2¾ in
   (6.8cm) [2⅛ in (5.5cm)]
Details in square brackets apply to the
   baby koala only. All other specifications are for both figures.

MATERIALS
Felting wool
 Natural blend: gray 15g [6g], small
    amount of graphite
Unbleached Shetland: small amount
Extras: solid black eyes, 4mm diameter
    x 1 set [3mm diameter x 1 set]
Have handy: awl, glue

Instructions
1. Create individual parts, referring
   to actual-size diagrams
2. Attach head to body
3. Attach front and hind legs to body.
   Add roving around the thighs to
   create fullness
4. Punch in white roving on the chest
5. Attach ears to head
6. Create face
7. Create claws on feet

<ACTUAL-SIZE PARTS>
○ Figures indicate number of parts required
Use gray unless otherwise indicated

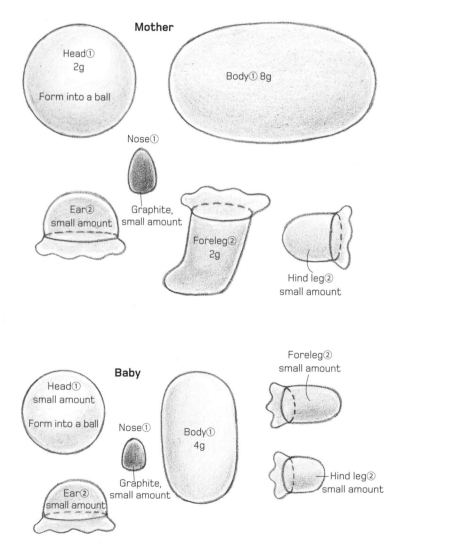

Mother

Head① 2g
Form into a ball

Body① 8g

Nose①

Ear② small amount

Graphite, small amount

Foreleg② 2g

Hind leg② small amount

Baby

Head① small amount
Form into a ball

Nose①

Graphite, small amount

Body① 4g

Ear② small amount

Foreleg② small amount

Hind leg② small amount

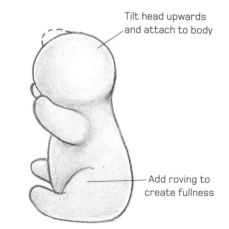

Add roving to create fullness

Tilt head upwards and attach to body

Add roving to create fullness

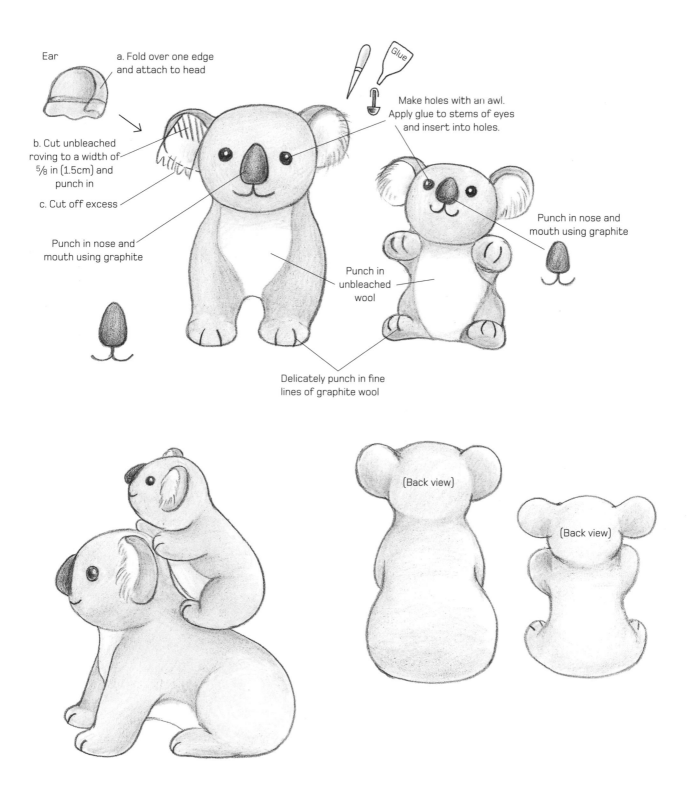

Ear

a. Fold over one edge and attach to head

b. Cut unbleached roving to a width of ⅝ in (1.5cm) and punch in

c. Cut off excess

Punch in nose and mouth using graphite

Glue

Make holes with an awl. Apply glue to stems of eyes and insert into holes.

Punch in unbleached wool

Punch in nose and mouth using graphite

Delicately punch in fine lines of graphite wool

(Back view)

(Back view)

AUSTRALIA
Mother Kangaroo and Joey

Page 10

Mother Kangaroo and Joey…height 4½ in (11.5cm) [1½ in (3.8cm)]
Details in square brackets apply to the joey only. All other specifications are for both figures.

MATERIALS
Felting wool
Natural blend: beige 18g, tan 3g
Solid: small amount of black
Extras: solid black eyes, 4mm diameter x 1 set [3mm diameter x 1 set]
Have handy: awl, glue

Instructions
1. Create individual parts, referring to actual-size diagrams
2. Attach head to body
3. Attach arms and legs to body. Work in beige roving around thighs and hips to create fullness
4. Add a light layer of tan roving over head, back, arms and legs and punch in
5. Attach ears to head
6. Create face (eyes, nose, mouth)
7. Attach tail to body
8. Create claws on front and hind paws
9. Attach pouch to belly
10. Create joey
11. Attach head and limbs to body and ears to head. Create face
12. Place joey in pouch

<ACTUAL-SIZE PARTS>
◯ Figures indicate number of parts required

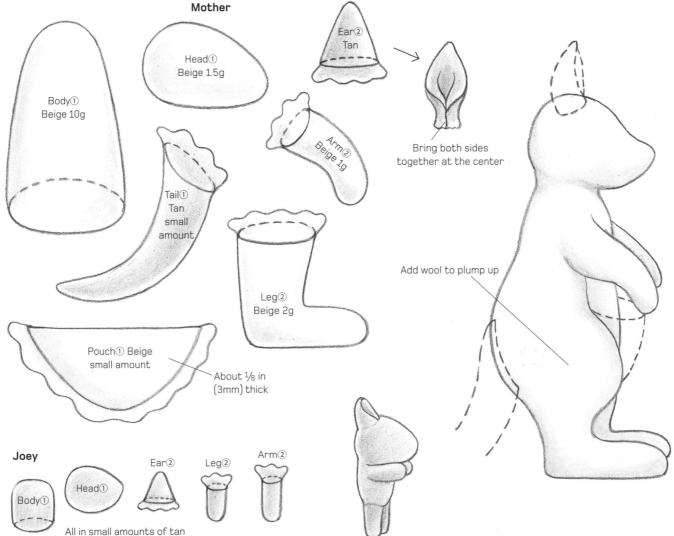

Mother

Body① Beige 10g

Head① Beige 1.5g

Ear② Tan

Bring both sides together at the center

Arm② Beige 1g

Tail① Tan small amount

Leg② Beige 2g

Pouch① Beige small amount

About ⅛ in (3mm) thick

Add wool to plump up

Joey

Body①

Head①

Ear②

Leg②

Arm②

All in small amounts of tan

50

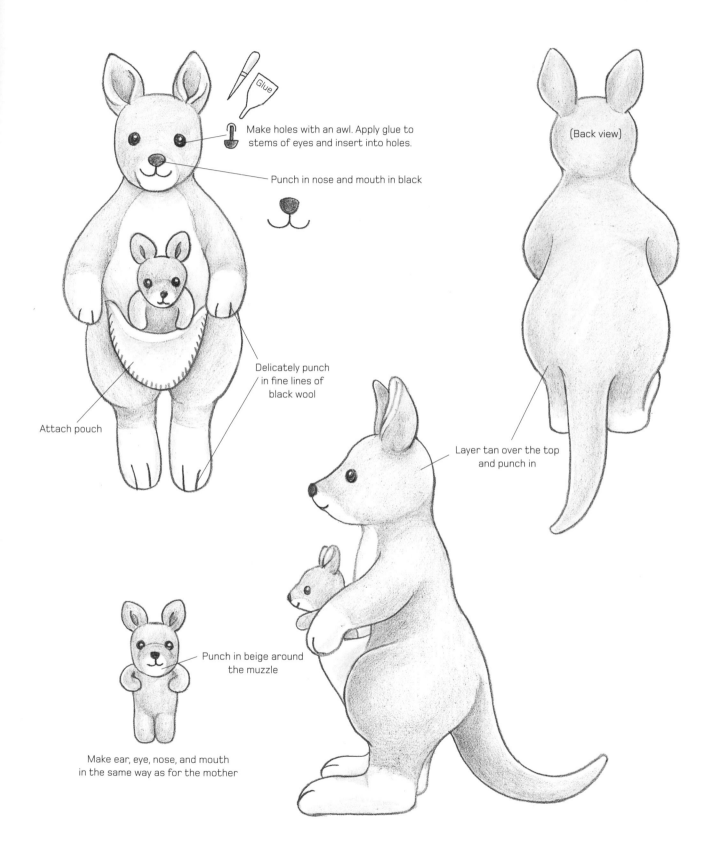

Make holes with an awl. Apply glue to stems of eyes and insert into holes.

Punch in nose and mouth in black

Delicately punch in fine lines of black wool

Attach pouch

Layer tan over the top and punch in

(Back view)

Punch in beige around the muzzle

Make ear, eye, nose, and mouth in the same way as for the mother

NEW ZEALAND
Sheep on a Hill

Page 11

Sheep on a Hill…height 1¾ in (4.5cm)

MATERIALS

Felting wool

Prefelted sheet, solid: French vanilla
9 x 5½ in (23x14cm), small amount
of soft green

Natural blend: beige 5g, small amount
of tan

Felting yarn, loop type: small amount of
unbleached

Extras: felting mat 6 x 6 in (15x15cm)

Black beads 2mm (size 11) x 6

Have handy: glue, trimmer, scissors,
sewing needle, thread

Instructions

1. Create base (see p36)
2. Create sheep (x3)
   a. Create individual parts, referring
      to actual-size diagrams
   b. Apply felting yarn to body sections
   c. Attach ears and legs
   d. Attach eyes
3. Glue sheep to base

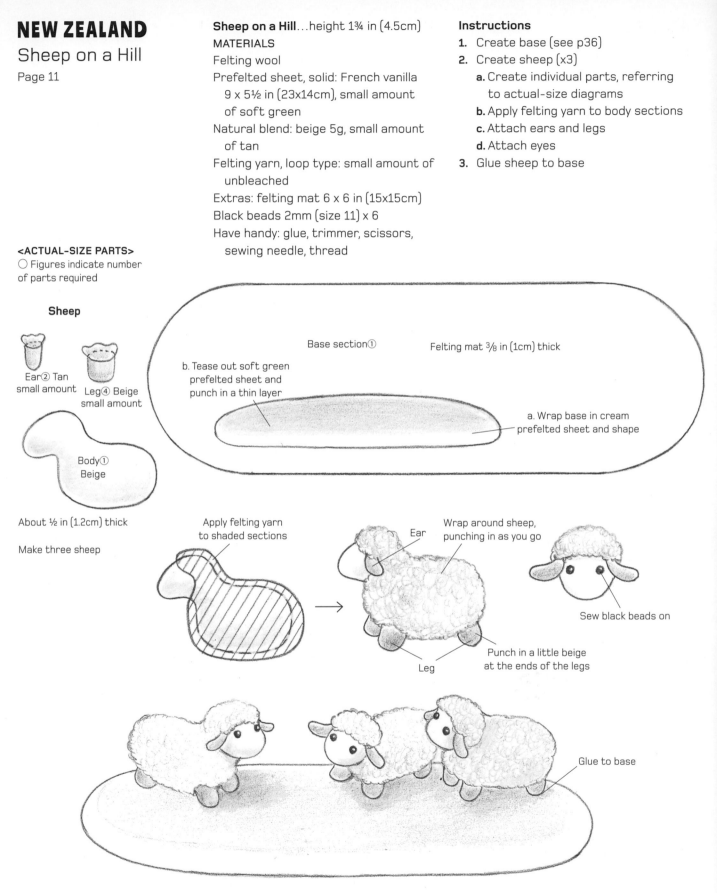

<ACTUAL-SIZE PARTS>
○ Figures indicate number
of parts required

Sheep

Ear② Tan
small amount

Leg④ Beige
small amount

Body① Beige

About ½ in (1.2cm) thick

Make three sheep

Base section①

Felting mat ⅜ in (1cm) thick

b. Tease out soft green prefelted sheet and punch in a thin layer

a. Wrap base in cream prefelted sheet and shape

Apply felting yarn to shaded sections

Ear

Wrap around sheep, punching in as you go

Sew black beads on

Leg

Punch in a little beige at the ends of the legs

Glue to base

52

RUSSIA
Four Matryoshka Maidens
Page 12

Matryoshka…height: large 2½ in (6.5cm); medium 2 in (5.2cm); small 1¾ in (4.5cm); tiny 1⅜ in (3.5cm)

MATERIALS—LARGE, TINY
Felting wool
Natural merino: white 14g
Mixed: small amounts of pink, rich brown, golden
Natural blend: small amounts of light salmon, blue green, soft orange
Solid: small amount of salmon

MATERIALS—MEDIUM
Felting wool
Natural merino: white 8g
Natural blend: small amounts of mint green, blue green, soft orange, cream, light salmon
Mixed: small amount of rich brown
Solid: small amount of salmon

MATERIALS—SMALL
Felting wool
Natural merino: white 4g
Mixed: small amounts of golden and rich brown
Solid: small amounts of lilac, purple, salmon
Natural blend: small amounts of blue green, soft orange, light salmon

Instructions
1. Use white roving to create the basic shape, with the actual-size diagrams for reference
2. Place scarf and clothes on the figure and punch in lightly
3. Punch in facial details (eyes, mouth, cheeks) and bangs
4. Punch in scarf knot detail
5. Punch in floral motif

<ACTUAL-SIZE>

Large

Make base in white 12g

Golden
Pink
White
Blue green
Light salmon
Rich brown
Pink
Rich brown
White
Salmon
Soft orange

Punch in fine layers of roving as if wrapping over the base shape

[Side view]

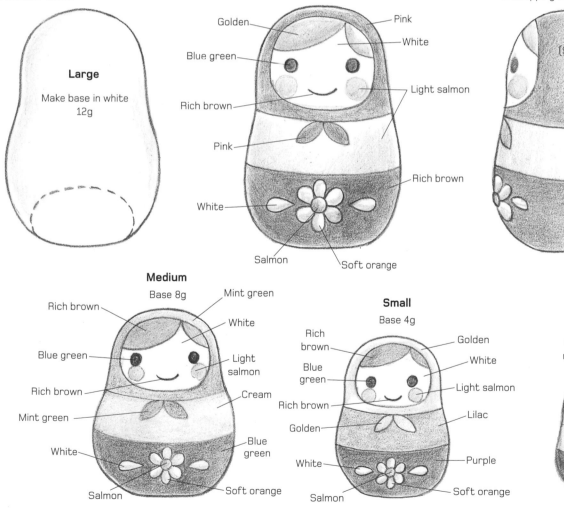

Medium
Base 8g
Rich brown
Mint green
White
Blue green
Light salmon
Rich brown
Cream
Mint green
White
Blue green
Salmon
Soft orange

Small
Base 4g
Rich brown
Golden
Blue green
White
Rich brown
Light salmon
Golden
Lilac
White
Purple
Salmon
Soft orange

Tiny
Base 2g
Use same type of roving as for large

USA
Hamburger and Donut Dangles

Page 13

Donut Dangle…cup height 1 in (2.5cm), donut height 1⅛ in (2.8cm)

MATERIALS

Felting wool

Solid: wheat 1.5g, small amounts of brown, pale pink, primary blue deep red, white

Extras: 1 star-shaped rhinestone, 5mm size

White seed beads 2mm (size 11) x 6

Strap cord, white and silver x 1

6mm double jump ring in silver x 1

Have handy: glue (for soda cup), scissors, sewing needle, thread

Hamburger Dangle…soda cup height 1⅜ in (3.5cm), hamburger height 1 in (2.5cm)

MATERIALS

Felting wool

Natural blend: goldenrod 1.5g

Solid: wheat 1.5g, small amounts of brown, primary blue, deep red, white and spring green

Mixed: small amounts of rich brown and chestnut

Extras: 1 star-shaped rhinestone, 5mm size

Strap cord, white and silver x 1

6mm double jump ring in silver x 1

Instructions

1. Create individual parts, referring to actual-size diagrams
2. Add roving around the top of the coffee and soda cups to form shape and punch in brown inside the cups
3. Referring to the diagrams of the finished projects, punch in required colors of roving to complete items
4. Connect parts with jump rings and attach strap cords (thread sewing needle and pass through the center of each part as shown on p40)

<ACTUAL-SIZE PARTS> ※Make parts firm

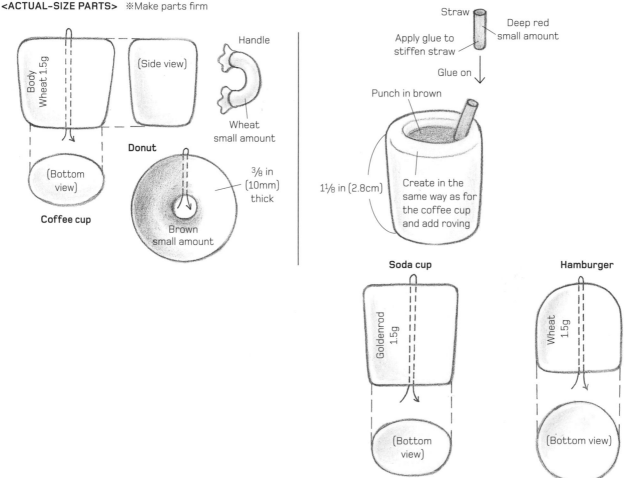

Add roving

Body of cup

1 in (2.5cm)

Punch in brown

Punch in handle

Primary blue

Deep red

White

Glue on rhinestone

Double jump ring

Pale pink

Sew on white seed beads

Strap cord

Double jump ring

Chestnut

Rich brown

Spring green

Deep red

Brown

Rich brown

Conceal knot with a little roving

55

MEXICO
Monkey with Maracas and Cactus
Page 14

Monkey…height 3⅞ in (9.8cm) with stump

MATERIALS
Felting wool

Natural blend: beige x 21g, goldenrod x 1.5g, small amount of tan

Mixed: small amounts of rich brown and moss

Solid: small amounts of deep red, salmon and brown

Extras: small amounts of no. 25 embroidery thread in salmon pink and soft green

Solid black eyes, 3mm diameter x 1 set

Have handy: awl, glue, sewing/embroidery needle

Instructions
1. Create individual parts, referring to actual-size diagrams
2. Attach head to body and shape while adding roving
3. Attach limbs to body
4. Punch in rich brown on limbs, body and head
5. Attach ears to head and create face (eyes, mouth, nose, cheeks)
6. Attach hat to head
7. Attach tail to body and finish off the ends of the limbs
8. Tie kerchief around neck and punch in
9. Apply glue to maracas and place in hands
10. Apply glue to bottom and seat monkey on tree stump

<ACTUAL-SIZE PARTS>
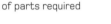 Figures indicate number of parts required

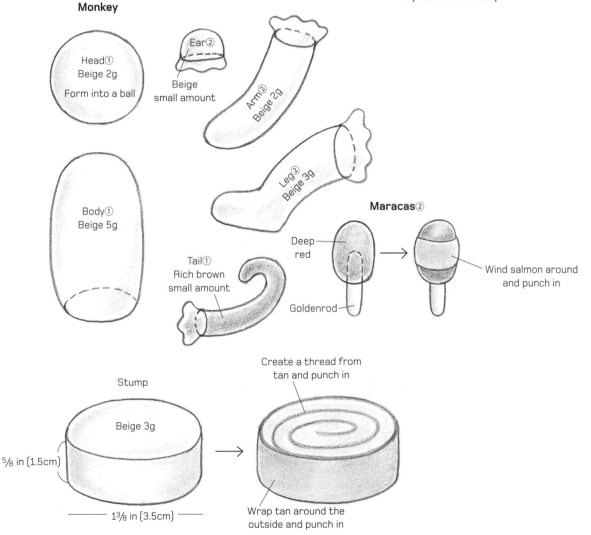

Monkey

Head① Beige 2g
Form into a ball

Ear②
Beige small amount

Arm② Beige 2g

Body① Beige 5g

Leg② Beige 3g

Tail①
Rich brown small amount

Maracas②

Deep red

Goldenrod

Wind salmon around and punch in

Stump

Beige 3g

⅝ in (1.5cm)

1⅜ in (3.5cm)

Create a thread from tan and punch in

Wrap tan around the outside and punch in

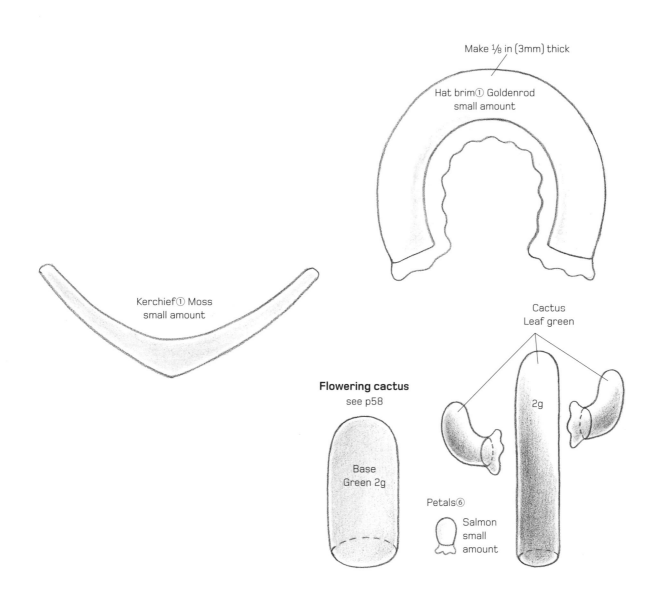

Make ⅛ in (3mm) thick

Hat brim① Goldenrod
small amount

Kerchief① Moss
small amount

Cactus
Leaf green

Flowering cactus
see p58

Base
Green 2g

2g

Petals⑥

Salmon
small
amount

Cactuses…height 2⅜ in (6cm)

Flowering cactus height 1⅝ in (4.2cm)

MATERIALS

Felting wool

Solid: leaf green x 3g, small amounts of salmon and white

Mixed: green x 2.5g, small amount of chestnut

Instructions

1. Create individual parts, referring to actual-size diagrams
2. Add roving to the flowering cactus base to create shape. Assemble parts of cactus
3. Create plant pots
4. Punch in flower for flowering cactus

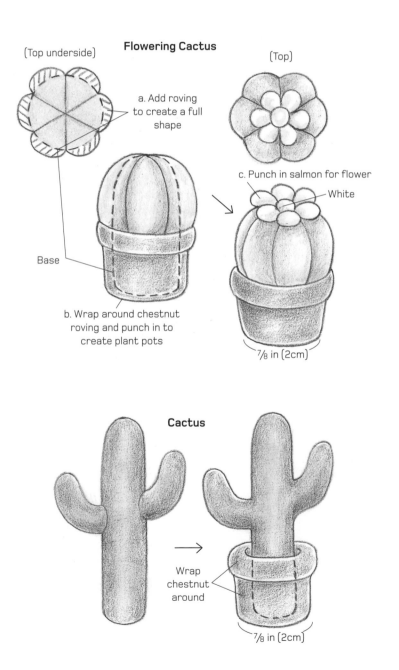

Flowering Cactus

(Top underside)

(Top)

a. Add roving to create a full shape

Base

b. Wrap around chestnut roving and punch in to create plant pots

c. Punch in salmon for flower

White

⅞ in (2cm)

Cactus

Wrap chestnut around

⅞ in (2cm)

Monkey

Attaching the hat

a. Punch in the brim around the head

b. Punch in goldenrod to cover the head

c. Embroider in two colors around the brim

Layer rich brown over the top and punch in

Tail

Make holes with an awl.
Apply glue to stems of eyes and insert into holes.

Glue on

Punch in thin lines of brown

Ear

Punch in thin layer of salmon

Punch in thin line of brown

Kerchief

Glue on

Stump

59

INDIA
Elephant on Festival Day
Page 16

Elephant…height 2¾ in (7cm) length 4⅜ in (11cm)

MATERIALS
Felting wool

Natural blend: gray x 30g

Solid: small amounts of rose, lemon yellow, deep red, pale pink and white

Extras: solid black eyes, 4mm diameter x 1 set

3mm rhinestones in red x 3

Have handy: awl, glue

Instructions
1. Create individual parts, referring to actual-size diagrams
2. Attach legs to body
3. Attach head to body
4. Attach trunk and tusks
5. Attach ears
6. Attach eyes
7. Attach tail
8. Attach decorations to back and head

<ACTUAL-SIZE PARTS>

○ Figures indicate number of parts required

Use gray unless otherwise indicated

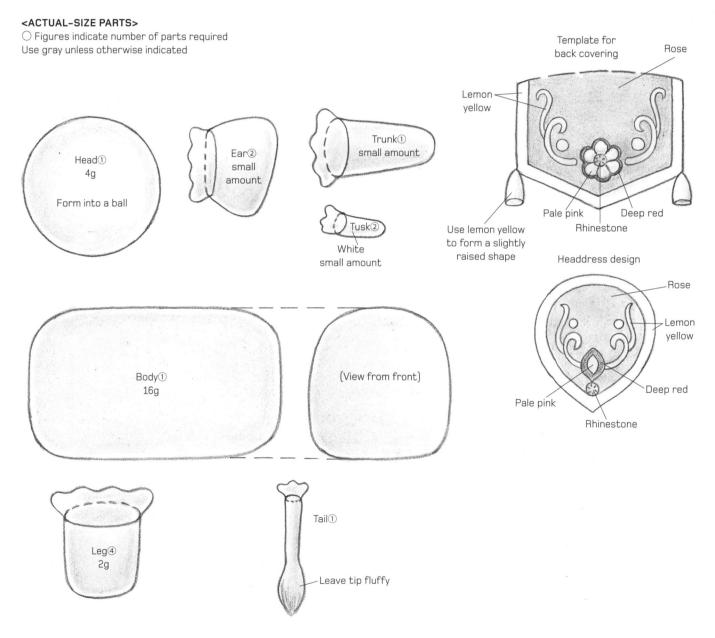

Head①
4g
Form into a ball

Ear②
small
amount

Trunk①
small amount

Tusk②
White
small amount

Template for back covering

Rose

Lemon yellow

Use lemon yellow to form a slightly raised shape

Pale pink

Rhinestone

Deep red

Headdress design

Rose

Lemon yellow

Deep red

Pale pink

Rhinestone

Body①
16g

(View from front)

Leg④
2g

Tail①

Leave tip fluffy

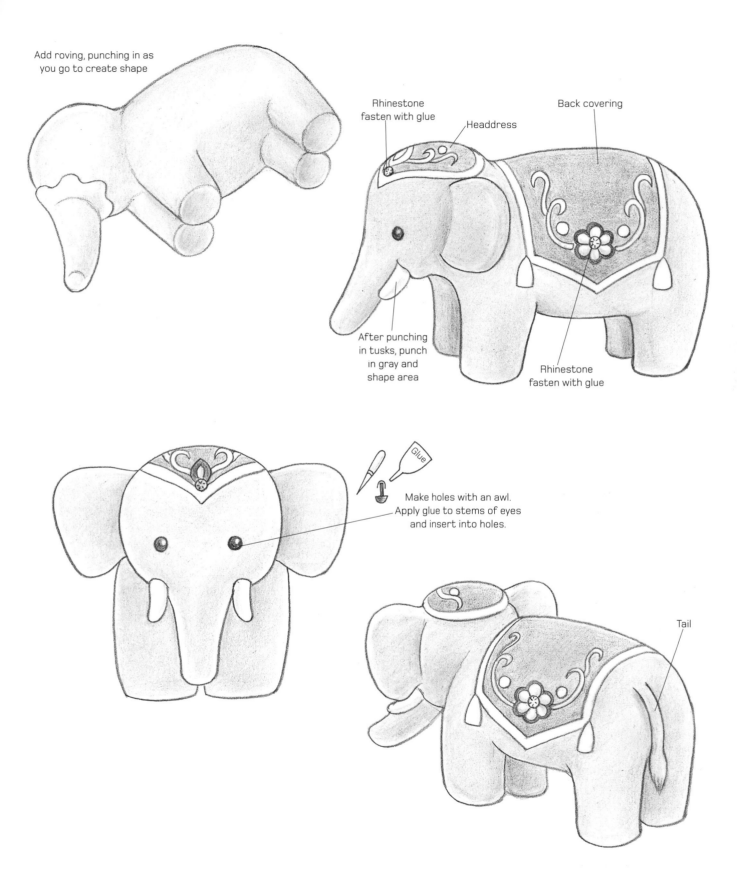

Add roving, punching in as you go to create shape

Rhinestone fasten with glue

Headdress

Back covering

After punching in tusks, punch in gray and shape area

Rhinestone fasten with glue

Glue

Make holes with an awl. Apply glue to stems of eyes and insert into holes.

Tail

PALAU
Tropical Fish Mobile
Page 18

Tropical Fish Mobile...length 11 in (28cm) (including fishing line)

MATERIALS for two 2-fish mobiles as shown on p18

Felting wool

Solid: white 8g, small amounts of orange yellow, black, dark orange, spring green, primary yellow, light blue, sky blue, deep red

Natural blend: small amount of blue green

Extras: Swarovski 8mm bicone beads in blue

Fine fishing line app 18 in (46cm) x 2

Have handy: sewing needle

Instructions

1. Create fish, fins and water drops referring to actual-size parts diagrams
2. Attach fins to fish base shapes
3. Layer color over fish and water drops to complete
4. Thread fishing line on to sewing needle and connect beads, fish and water drops

Fish heights:
large: 1 in (2.5cm)
medium: ¾ in (1.9cm)
small: ⅝ in (1.5cm)

<ACTUAL-SIZE PARTS>
○ Figures indicate number of parts required

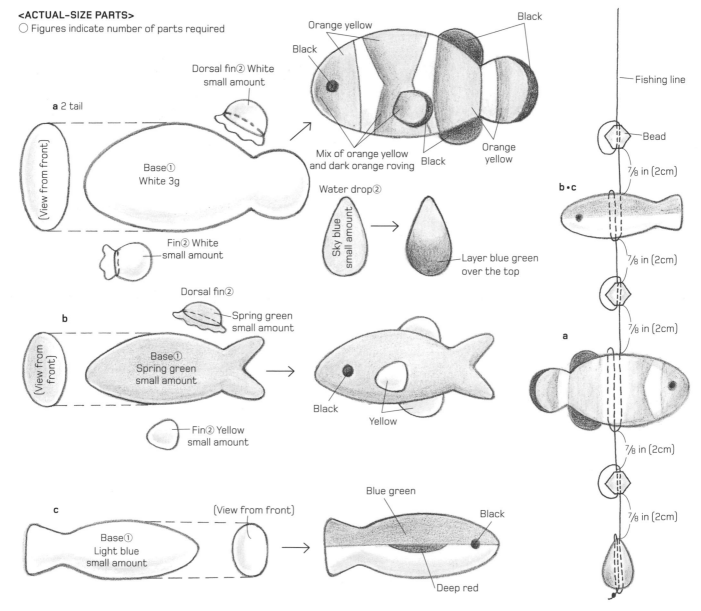

a 2 tail

(View from front)

Base① White 3g

Dorsal fin② White small amount

Fin② White small amount

Orange yellow

Black

Black

Mix of orange yellow and dark orange roving

Black

Orange yellow

Water drop②

Sky blue small amount

Layer blue green over the top

b

(View from front)

Base① Spring green small amount

Dorsal fin②

Spring green small amount

Fin② Yellow small amount

Black

Yellow

c

Base① Light blue small amount

(View from front)

Blue green

Black

Deep red

Fishing line

Bead

⅞ in (2cm)

b・c

⅞ in (2cm)

⅞ in (2cm)

a

⅞ in (2cm)

⅞ in (2cm)

62

ITALY
Rabbit Gondolier and His Gondola

Page 22

Rabbit Gondolier and Gondola...rabbit height 3¼ in (8.5cm), gondola 1⅝ in (4cm)

MATERIALS

Felting wool

Unbleached Shetland x 6g

Natural blend: brown x 7g, small amount of tan, light salmon, goldenrod and blue green

Solid: small amounts of pale green, green, deep red, light blue

Mixed: small amount of rich brown

Extras: solid black eyes, 3mm diameter x 1 set

Bamboo skewer x 1

Commercial felt, brown, 1¾ x 1 in (4.5x2.5cm)

⅜ in (10mm) wide linen-blend lace x 9.5 in (24cm)

Have handy: awl, glue, sewing needle, thread, scissors

Instructions

1. Create individual parts, referring to actual-size diagrams
2. Create gondola (see diagram)
3. Create rabbit
   a. Attach head to body
   b. Attach limbs to body
   c. Attach ears and create face
   d. Punch in stripes for shirt and wind kerchief around neck
   e. Finish off hands and feet
   f. Attach tail
   g. Create oars and use glue to place in hands
4. Use glue to secure rabbit to the mat inside the gondola
5. Create small bird and glue to prow of gondola

<ACTUAL–SIZE PARTS>
○ Figures indicate number of parts required
Use unbleached unless otherwise indicated

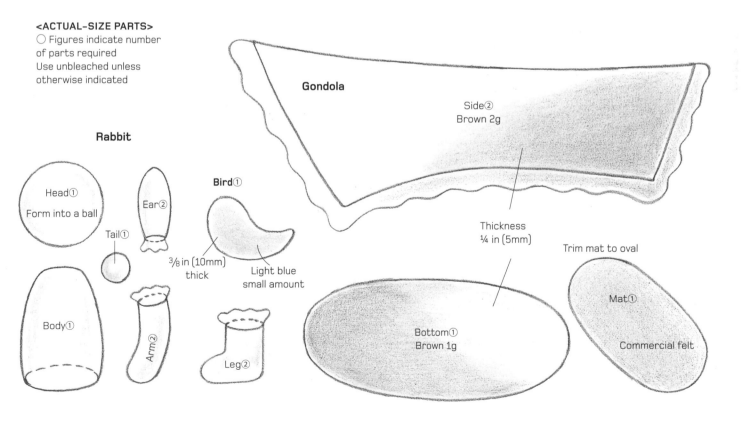

Rabbit

Head① Form into a ball

Tail①

Ear②

⅜ in (10mm) thick

Bird①

Light blue small amount

Body①

Arm②

Leg②

Gondola

Side② Brown 2g

Thickness ¼ in (5mm)

Bottom① Brown 1g

Trim mat to oval

Mat①

Commercial felt

63

Assembling the gondola

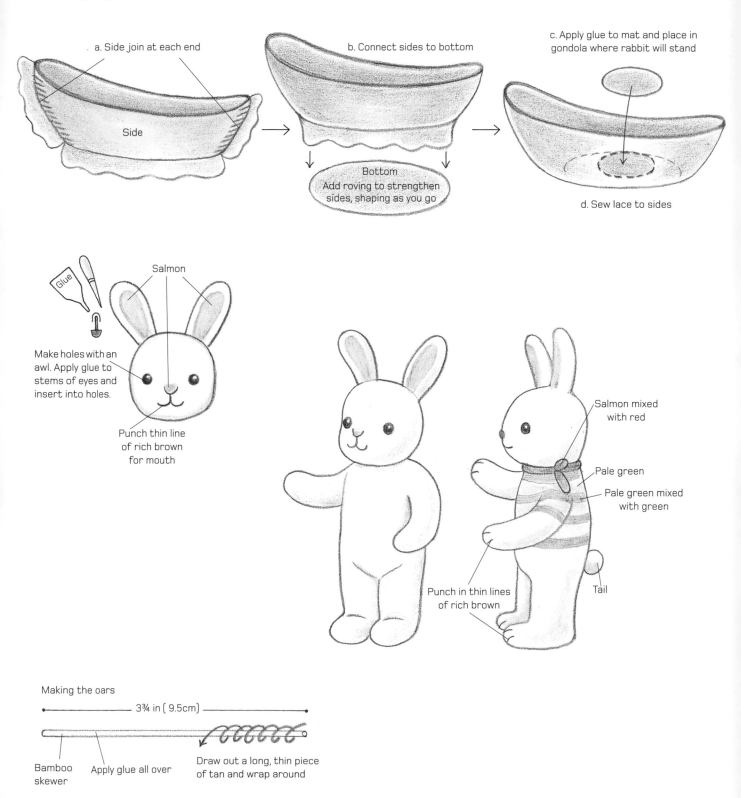

a. Side join at each end

Side

b. Connect sides to bottom

Bottom
Add roving to strengthen
sides, shaping as you go

c. Apply glue to mat and place in
gondola where rabbit will stand

d. Sew lace to sides

Glue

Make holes with an
awl. Apply glue to
stems of eyes and
insert into holes.

Salmon

Punch thin line
of rich brown
for mouth

Salmon mixed
with red

Pale green

Pale green mixed
with green

Punch in thin lines
of rich brown

Tail

Making the oars

3¾ in (9.5cm)

Bamboo
skewer

Apply glue all over

Draw out a long, thin piece
of tan and wrap around

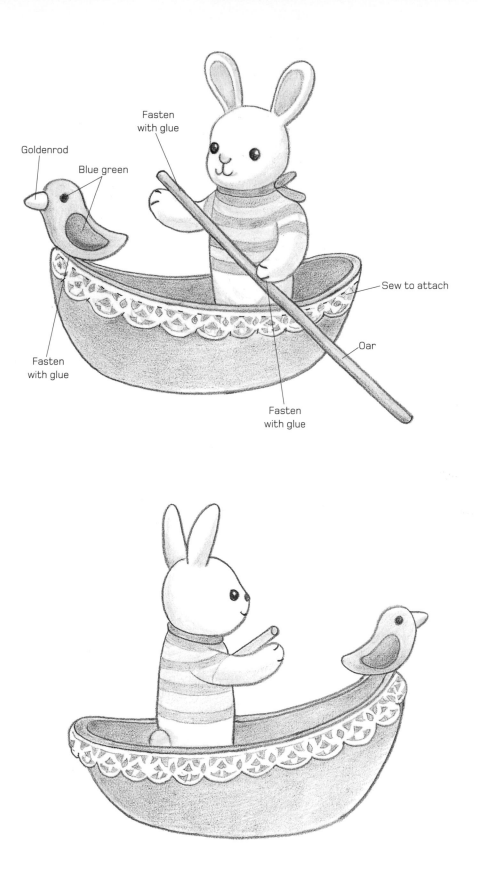

Goldenrod

Blue green

Fasten
with glue

Fasten
with glue

Sew to attach

Oar

Fasten
with glue

FINLAND
Santa Claus with Gifts
Page 24

Santa Claus...height 4¾ in (12cm)
MATERIALS
Felting wool
Batting 4g
Solid: deep red 12g, white 2g, leaf green
  2g, small amounts of black and salmon
Natural blend: cream 3g
Extras: gold cord 9½ in (24cm)
Have handy: glue, scissors

Instructions
1. Create individual parts, referring to actual-size diagrams
2. Attach head to body
3. Work white around wrists to create cuff
4. Punch in black on legs to create boots, working white around the cuffs
5. Attach limbs to body
6. Attach white trim to front and hems of jacket
7. Punch in deep red on head to create hat, working in the white trim before adding the tip of the hat. Attach pom pom to tip of hat.
8. Attach ears and create face (beard, brows, eyes, nose, cheeks)
9. Place gift box in Santa's hands

<ACTUAL-SIZE PARTS>
◯ Figures indicate number of parts required

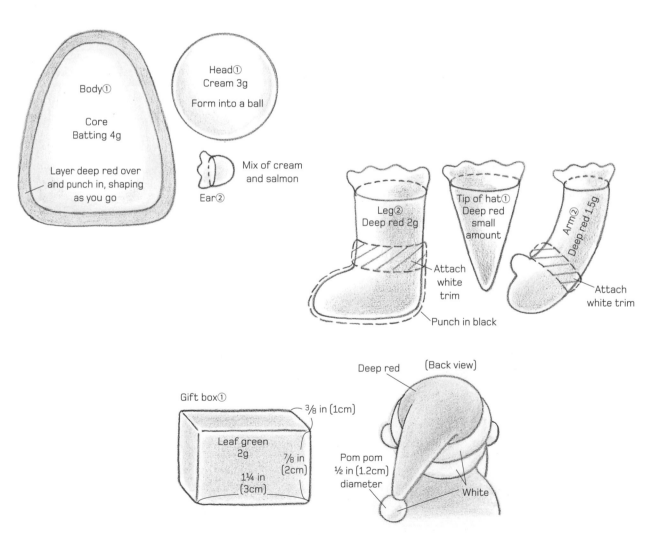

Body①

Core
Batting 4g

Layer deep red over and punch in, shaping as you go

Head①
Cream 3g

Form into a ball

Mix of cream and salmon

Ear②

Leg②
Deep red 2g

Attach white trim

Punch in black

Tip of hat①
Deep red small amount

Arm② Deep red 1.5g

Attach white trim

Gift box①

Leaf green 2g

⅜ in (1cm)

⅞ in (2cm)

1¼ in (3cm)

Deep red

(Back view)

Pom pom ½ in (1.2cm) diameter

White

Attaching the beard

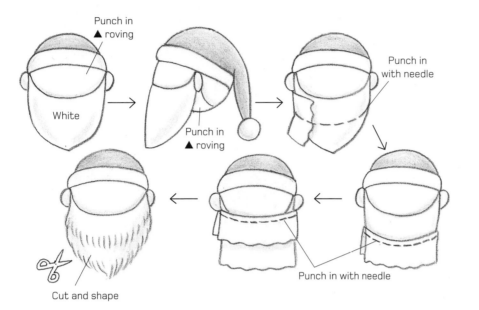

Punch in ▲ roving

White

Punch in ▲ roving

Punch in with needle

Punch in with needle

Cut and shape

Fasten with glue

White

Tie gold cord in a bow

<ACTUAL-SIZE>

White

Black

Salmon

Nose

Make a
ball from
▲ roving

White

Sack of Gifts…height 3⅜ in (8.5cm)

MATERIALS

Felting wool

Batting x 3g

Solid: white x 6g, small amounts of,
lilac, deep red, leaf green and black

Natural blend: small amounts of tan
and light salmon

Extras: small amount of no. 25
embroidery thread in purple

Red cord x 9 in (23cm)

Star-shaped rhinestone, 7mm size,
x 1

Have handy: glue, scissors

Instructions

1. Create individual parts, referring
   to actual-size diagrams
2. Attach edge to sack
3. Create presents
4. Place presents in sack and fasten with glue
5. Tie red cord around sack in a
   bow

<FULL-SCALE PARTS>

Gift Sack

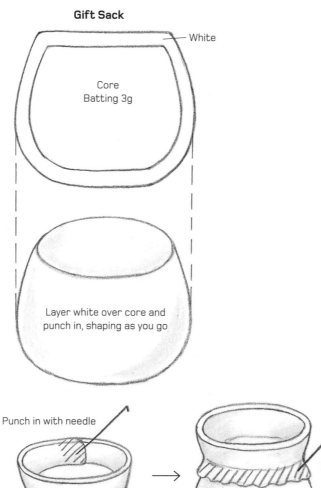

White

Core
Batting 3g

Layer white over core and
punch in, shaping as you go

Punch in with needle

Bring ends of sack edge
together to form ring

Punch with needle
to smooth out

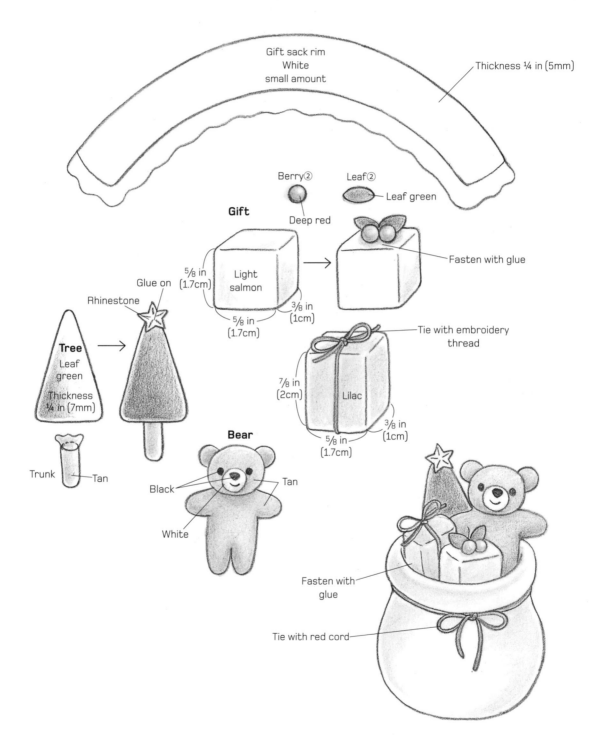

Gift sack rim
White
small amount

Thickness ¼ in (5mm)

Berry②

Leaf②

Leaf green

Deep red

Gift

Fasten with glue

⁵⁄₈ in (1.7cm)

Light salmon

³⁄₈ in (1cm)

⁵⁄₈ in (1.7cm)

Glue on

Rhinestone

Tie with embroidery thread

Tree
Leaf green

Thickness ¼ in (7mm)

⁷⁄₈ in (2cm)

Lilac

³⁄₈ in (1cm)

⁵⁄₈ in (1.7cm)

Trunk

Tan

Bear

Black

Tan

White

Fasten with glue

Tie with red cord

FINLAND
Little House in Spring and Winter
Page 26

House (Winter)…height 1¾ in (4.5cm) length 4⅛ in (10.5cm)

MATERIALS

Felting wool

Prefelted sheet, solid: white 7 x 6¾ in (18x17cm)

Prefelted sheet, natural mix: beige 14¼ x 8 in (36x20cm)

Solid: small amounts of brown, leaf green, black, deep red

Natural blend: small amount of tan

Mixed: small amount of chestnut

Extras: felting mat 6¼ x 4 in (16x10cm)

Star-shaped rhinestone x 1

White craft/decor sand

House (Spring)…height 1¾ in (4.5cm) length 4⅛ in (10.5cm)

MATERIALS

Felting wool

Prefelted sheet, solid: soft green 7 x 6¾ in (18x17cm)

Prefelted sheet, natural mix: beige 14¼ x 8 in (36x20cm)

Natural blend: small amounts of tan, brown

Solid: small amounts of green, moss green, pale yellow, deep brown

Mixed: small amount of moss

Extras: felting mat 6¼ x 4 in (16x10cm)

Small amounts of no. 25 embroidery thread in pink and white

Have handy: glue, trimmer, scissors, small cup, small craft brush, small amount water, sewing/ embroidery needle

Instructions

1. Create individual parts, referring to actual-size diagrams
2. Create base by wrapping in white for winter and soft green for spring (see p36)
3. Create house
4. Glue each part on to base
5. For the winter house, apply diluted glue to the roof, chimney and fir trees and sprinkle sand over them to represent snow

<ACTUAL-SIZE PARTS>
Make for both winter and spring
unless otherwise indicated

Create base of house from felting mat

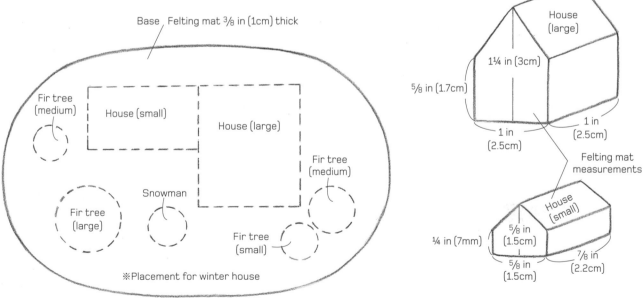

Winter

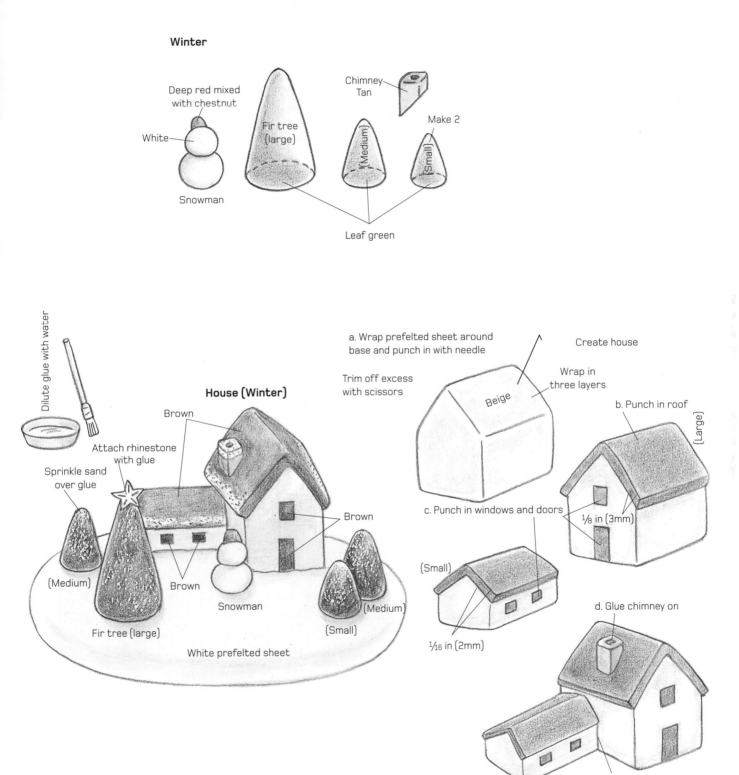

Deep red mixed with chestnut

White

Snowman

Fir tree (large)

(Medium)

(Small)

Chimney Tan

Make 2

Leaf green

Dilute glue with water

House (Winter)

Brown

Attach rhinestone with glue

Sprinkle sand over glue

Brown

(Medium)

Brown

Snowman

(Medium)

(Small)

Fir tree (large)

White prefelted sheet

a. Wrap prefelted sheet around base and punch in with needle

Trim off excess with scissors

Create house

Wrap in three layers

Beige

b. Punch in roof

(Large)

c. Punch in windows and doors

1/8 in (3mm)

(Small)

d. Glue chimney on

1/16 in (2mm)

e. Glue small and large houses together

71

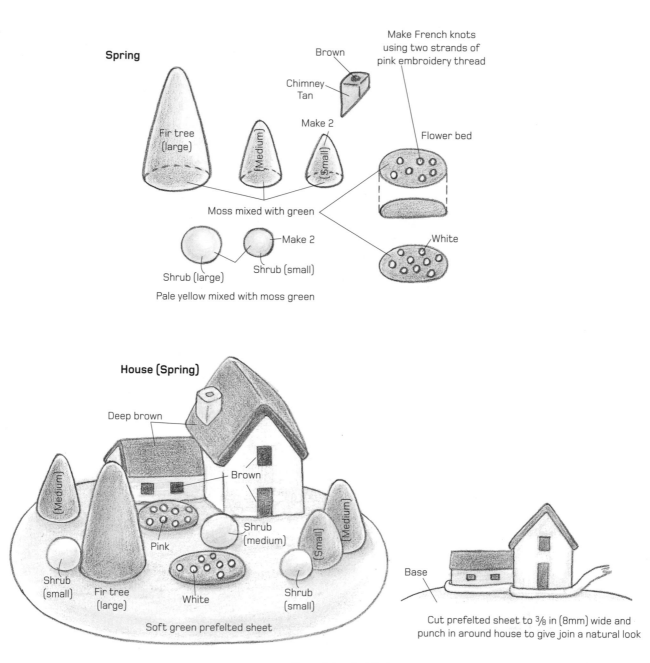

Spring

Brown

Chimney
Tan

Make 2

Make French knots
using two strands of
pink embroidery thread

Flower bed

Fir tree
(large)

(Medium)

(Small)

Make 2

Moss mixed with green

White

Shrub (large)

Shrub (small)

Pale yellow mixed with moss green

House (Spring)

Deep brown

Brown

Shrub
(medium)

(Medium)

Pink

(Small)

(Medium)

Shrub
(small)

Fir tree
(large)

White

Shrub
(small)

Soft green prefelted sheet

Base

Cut prefelted sheet to ⅜ in (8mm) wide and
punch in around house to give join a natural look

French knot stitch

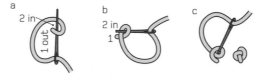

a
2 in
1 out

b
2 in
1

c

GERMANY
Teddy Bears and Castle
Page 28

Tan Teddy Bear…height 3¾ in (9.5cm)
MATERIALS
Felting wool
Natural blend: tan 18g, small amount of
brown
Solid: small amount of black
Extras: solid black eyes, 4.5mm diameter
x 1 set
Fine cord in brown x 10 in (25cm) and
chestnut x 10 in (25cm)
Have handy: awl, glue, scissors

Instructions (see also pp38–39)
1. Create actual-size parts
2. Attach head to body
3. Attach limbs
4. Attach muzzle to face and create
   face (eyes, nose, mouth)
5. Attach ears
6. Finish off hands and feet
7. Tie cord in a ribbon around neck and
   trim any excess

<ACTUAL-SIZE PARTS>
○ Figures indicate number of parts required
Use tan unless otherwise indicated
For the brown teddy bear, use brown to replace
tan and tan to replace brown

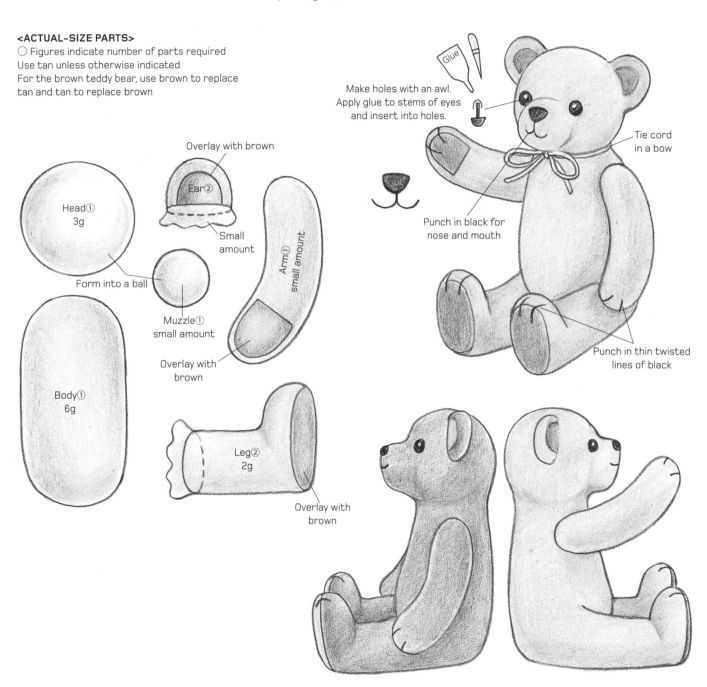

Overlay with brown

Ear②

Small amount

Head①
3g

Form into a ball

Muzzle①
small amount

Overlay with
brown

Arm①
small amount

Overlay with brown

Body①
6g

Leg②
2g

Overlay with
brown

Make holes with an awl.
Apply glue to stems of eyes
and insert into holes.

Glue

Tie cord
in a bow

Punch in black for
nose and mouth

Tie cord
in a bow

Punch in thin twisted
lines of black

Castle…height 3 in (7.8cm) length
 3¾ in (9.5cm)

MATERIALS

Felting wool

Prefelted sheet, solid: soft green
 6¼ x 6¾ in (16x17cm)

Prefelted sheet, natural mix:
 unbleached 12 x 12 in (30x30cm)

Natural blend: small amount of brown

Solid: small amount of leaf green

Mixed: small amount of moss

Extras: felting mat 6 x 2¾ in (15x7cm)

Have handy: glue, trimmer, scissors

Instructions (see also pp36–37)

1. Create base shape, referring to actual-size diagrams
2. Wrap prefelted sheet around base shape to create base
3. Create four parts of castle
4. Glue four parts together
5. Apply glue to bottom of castle and attach to base
6. Create greenery around castle

<ACTUAL–SIZE PARTS>

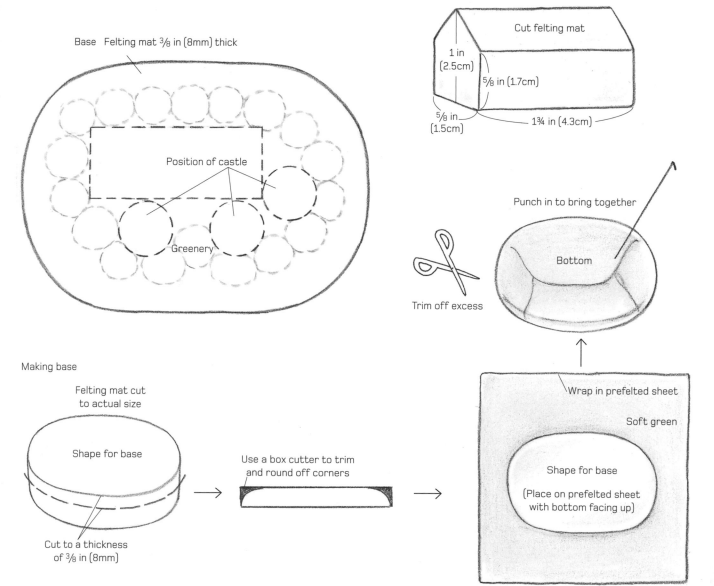

Base   Felting mat ⅜ in (8mm) thick

Position of castle

Greenery

Cut felting mat

1 in (2.5cm)

⅝ in (1.7cm)

⅝ in (1.5cm)

1¾ in (4.3cm)

Punch in to bring together

Bottom

Trim off excess

Making base

Felting mat cut to actual size

Shape for base

Cut to a thickness of ⅜ in (8mm)

Use a box cutter to trim and round off corners

Wrap in prefelted sheet

Soft green

Shape for base

(Place on prefelted sheet with bottom facing up)

Prefelted sheet unbleached

2 in (5cm)

Trim away corners

1¾ in (4.5cm)

⅝ in (1.5cm)

▲ ▲ △

3⁄8 in (1cm)

Use scissors to cut one cylinder only

Punch in brown

(Cross section)

Brown

(Top)

Fasten with glue

● ▲ △ ▲

a. Wrap in unbleached prefelted sheet and punch in. Do this three times in total, creating three layers (trim off excess).

●

b. Punch in brown

Greenery

Mix moss and leaf green, form into fluffy balls and punch in around castle.

Make about 18

½ in (1.3cm)

CANADA
Bear in the Forest

Page 27

Bear in the Forest…height 2⅜ in (6cm)
length 5¾ in (14.5cm)

MATERIALS

Felting wool

Prefelted sheet, natural mix: beige 8 x 6 in (20x15cm), camel 6 x 2⅜ in (15x6cm)

Solid: green 4g, small amount of deep brown and black

Natural blend: brown 3g

Extras: felting mat 6 x 2 in (15x6cm)

Seed beads in black 2mm (size 11) x 2

Have handy: glue, trimmer, scissors, sewing needle, thread

Instructions

1. Create base (see p36)
2. Create individual parts, referring to actual-size diagrams
3. Create five trees, attaching trunks to greenery with glue
4. Create bear
   a. Attach head to body
   b. Attach legs to body
   c. Attach ears and create face
   d. Attach tail
5. Glue trees and bear to base

<ACTUAL-SIZE PARTS>

○ Figures indicate number of parts required

Use small amounts of brown unless otherwise indicated

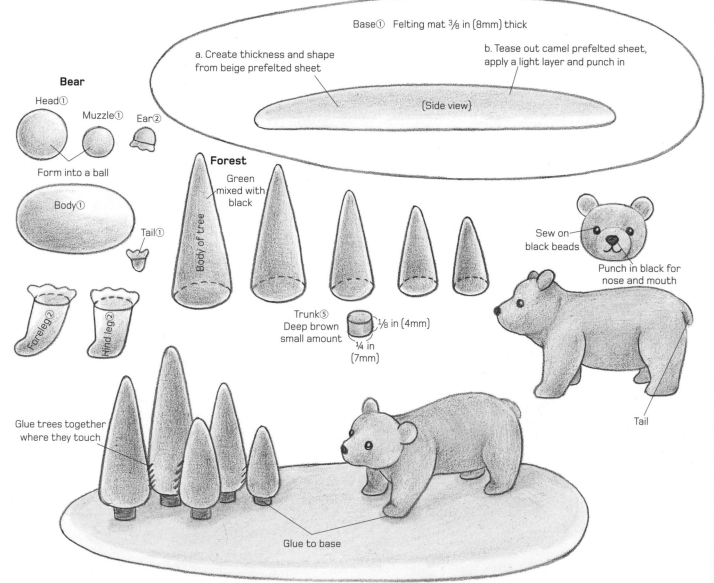

Base① Felting mat ⅜ in (8mm) thick

a. Create thickness and shape from beige prefelted sheet

b. Tease out camel prefelted sheet, apply a light layer and punch in

(Side view)

Bear

Head①

Muzzle①

Ear②

Form into a ball

Body①

Tail①

Foreleg②

Hind leg②

Forest

Green mixed with black

Body of tree

Trunk⑤
Deep brown small amount

⅛ in (4mm)

¼ in (7mm)

Sew on black beads

Punch in black for nose and mouth

Tail

Glue trees together where they touch

Glue to base

FRANCE
Paris Dangle
Page 30

Eiffel Tower Dangle…height 2¼ in (5.5cm)
MATERIALS
Felting wool
Natural blend: gray 2g, small amount of graphite
Solid: small amounts of white , primary blue, deep red
Extras: strap cord in white and silver x 1

Have handy: strong sewing needle, thread, scissors

Baguette Dangle…height 2¼ in (5.5cm)
MATERIALS
Felting wool
Solid: small amounts of wheat, white, primary blue, deep red
Mixed: small amount of chestnut
Natural blend: small amount of tan
Extras: strap cord in white and silver x 1

All instructions for these dangles are in the diagrams below

<ACTUAL-SIZE PARTS>
Make parts firm

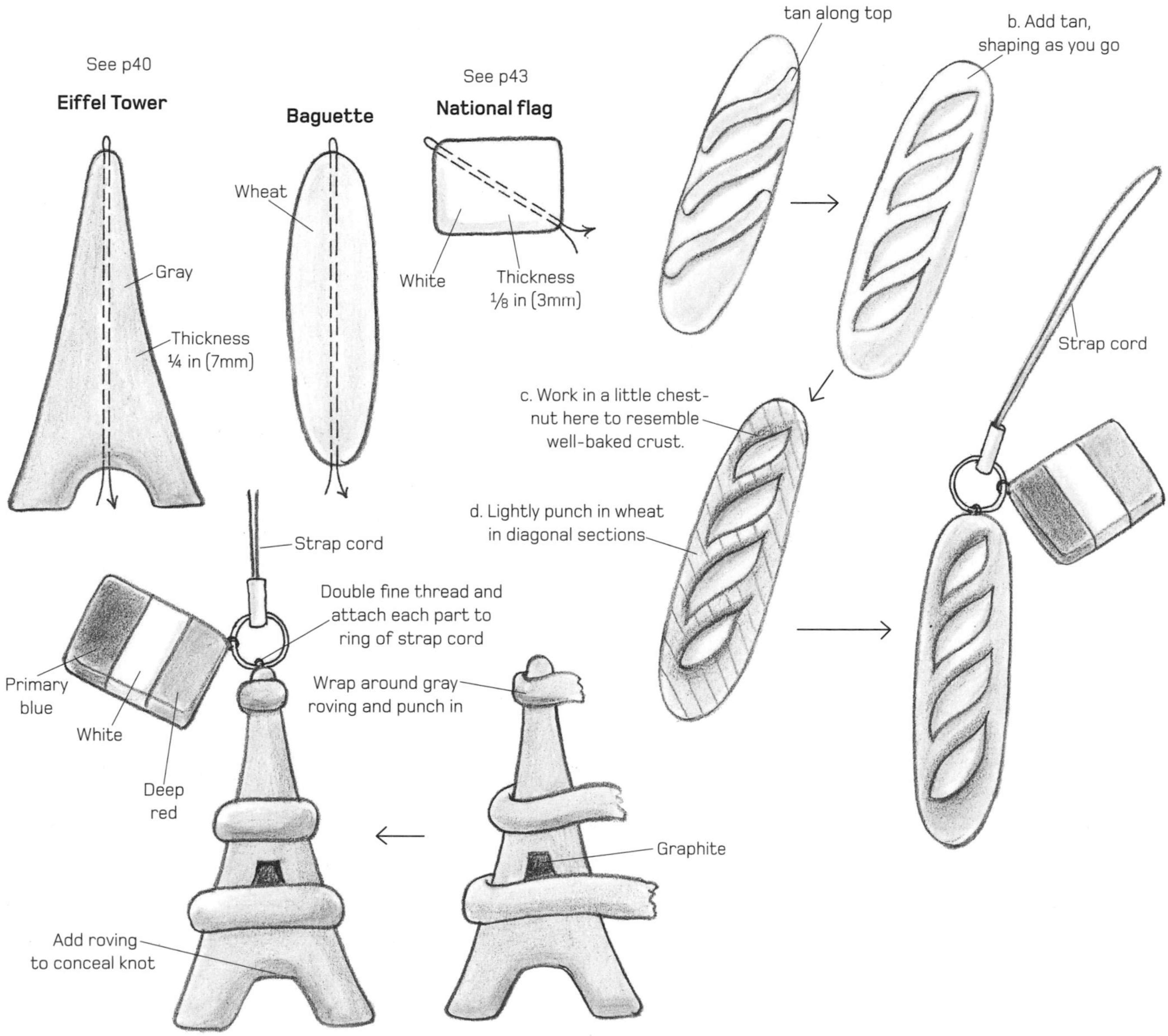

See p40
Eiffel Tower

Gray

Thickness ¼ in (7mm)

Baguette

Wheat

See p43
National flag

White

Thickness ⅛ in (3mm)

a. Punch in tan along top

b. Add tan, shaping as you go

Strap cord

c. Work in a little chestnut here to resemble well-baked crust.

d. Lightly punch in wheat in diagonal sections

Strap cord

Double fine thread and attach each part to ring of strap cord

Wrap around gray roving and punch in

Primary blue

White

Deep red

Graphite

Add roving to conceal knot

77

UNITED KINGDOM
London Dangles
Page 31

Fox Terrier Dangle…height 2¼ in (5.5cm)

MATERIALS

Felting wool

Solid: white 3g, small amounts of brown,
  deep red, primary blue

Mixed: small amount of rich brown

Extras: strap cord in black and gold x 1

Queen's Guard Dangle…height 2½ in (6cm)

MATERIALS

Felting wool

Natural blend: cream x 4g

Mixed: small amount of rich brown

Solid: deep red x 2g, small amounts
  of black, white, navy, pale pink

Extras: strap cord in black and gold x 1

Have handy: strong sewing needle,
  thread, scissors

Instructions
Fox Terrier and National Flag
1. Create individual parts, referring to actual-size diagrams
2. Create markings by working in first brown, then rich brown and attach ears
3. Work in line patterns on flag

Queen's Guard and Bus
1. Create individual parts, referring to actual-size diagrams
2. Add roving to base shape of guard to create form and attach legs
3. Add roving for hat, hair, face and clothes and punch in
4. Punch in windows and lines on bus and attach wheels

For Both Straps
Double sewing thread and attach each part to ring of strap cord. Add roving to cover knot (see p40).

<ACTUAL-SIZE PARTS>
○ Figures indicate number of parts required
Make parts firm

See p43 for flag base

National Flag
Primary blue
Thickness ¼ in (5mm)

Ear② — Brown

Fox terrier
White 3g
Thickness ⅜ in (1cm)

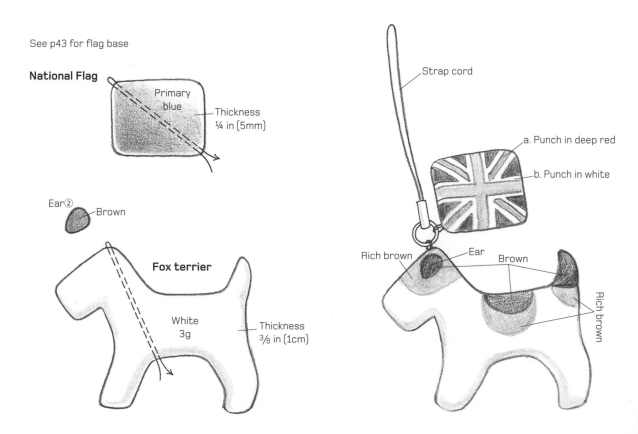

Strap cord

a. Punch in deep red

b. Punch in white

Rich brown

Ear

Brown

Rich brown

Queen's Guard

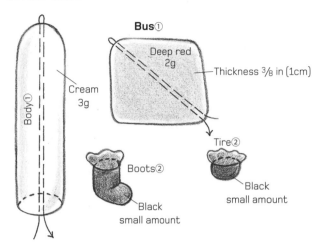

Body①

Cream
3g

Bus①

Deep red
2g

Thickness ³⁄₈ in (1cm)

Tire②

Black
small amount

Boots②

Black
small amount

Cover with cream roving
and form upper body

Body

Boots

Rich brown

White

Strap cord

Tire

Black

Navy blue

Pale pink

Rich brown

Deep red

White

Published by Tuttle Publishing, an imprint of Periplus Editions (HK) Ltd.

www.tuttlepublishing.com

ISBN 978-4-8053-1436-4

Felt Youmou de Meguru Chiisana Sekai Ryokou (NV70039)
Copyright © Sachiko Susa / NIHON VOGUE-SHA 2010
All rights reserved.
Photographer: Toshikatsu Watanabe
English translation rights arranged with NIHON VOGUE CO., LTD.
through Japan UNI Agency, Inc., Tokyo

English Translation © 2016 Periplus Editions (HK) Ltd.
Translated from Japanese by Leeyong Soo

Distributed by

North America, Latin America & Europe
Tuttle Publishing
364 Innovation Drive, North Clarendon
VT 05759-9436 U.S.A.
Tel: 1 (802) 773-8930
Fax: 1 (802) 773-6993
info@tuttlepublishing.com
www.tuttlepublishing.com

Japan
Tuttle Publishing
Yaekari Building, 3rd Floor
5-4-12 Osaki
Shinagawa-ku
Tokyo 141 0032
Tel: (81) 3 5437-0171
Fax: (81) 3 5437-0755
sales@tuttle.co.jp
www.tuttle.co.jp

Asia Pacific
Berkeley Books Pte. Ltd.
61 Tai Seng Avenue #02-12
Singapore 534167
Tel: (65) 6280-1330
Fax: (65) 6280-6290
inquiries@periplus.com.sg
www.periplus.com

Printed in China   1611RR
19 18 17 16   10 9 8 7 6 5 4 3 2 1

TUTTLE PUBLISHING® is a registered trademark of Tuttle Publishing, a division of Periplus Editions (HK) Ltd.

About Tuttle
"Books to Span the East and West"

Our core mission at Tuttle Publishing is to create books which bring people together one page at a time. Tuttle was founded in 1832 in the small New England town of Rutland, Vermont (USA). Our fundamental values remain as strong today as they were then—to publish best-in-class books informing the English-speaking world about the countries and peoples of Asia. The world has become a smaller place today and Asia's economic, cultural and political influence has expanded, yet the need for meaningful dialogue and information about this diverse region has never been greater. Since 1948, Tuttle has been a leader in publishing books on the cultures, arts, cuisines, languages and literatures of Asia. Our authors and photographers have won numerous awards and Tuttle has published thousands of books on subjects ranging from martial arts to paper crafts. We welcome you to explore the wealth of information available on Asia at **www.tuttlepublishing.com.**